# ANSWER

## ONE OF THESE BOTTLE'S IS IN EVERY IMAGE –

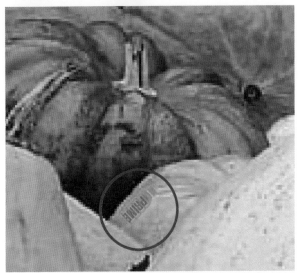

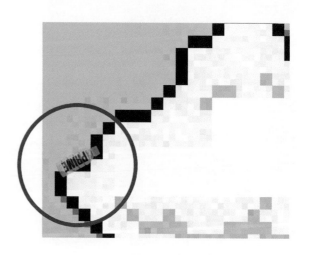

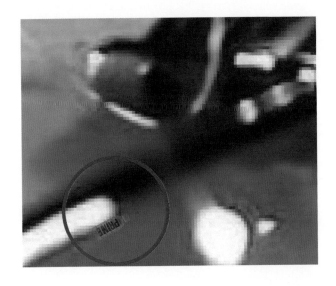
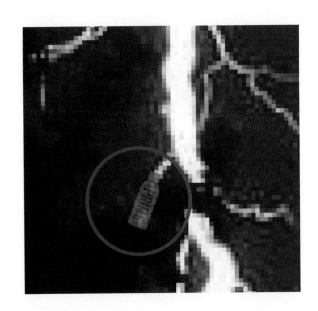
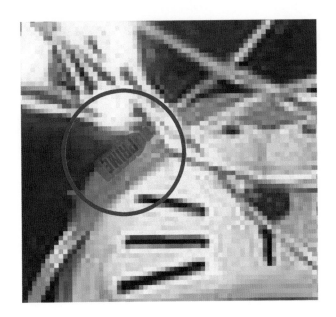

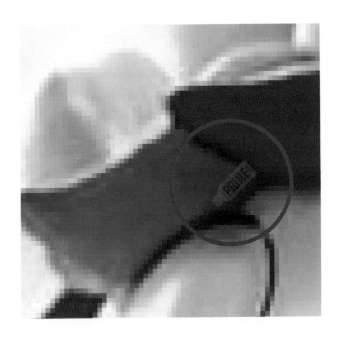
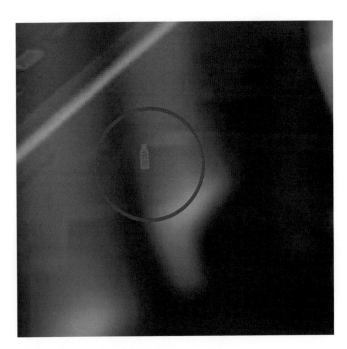

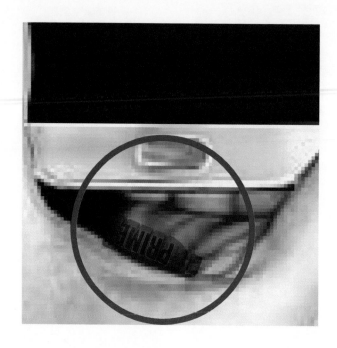

For more Prime products please visit our Facebook page 'Project Publishing'

You'll find Prime colouring books and notebooks of all designs that are being enjoyed all around the World.

Printed in Great Britain
by Amazon

35465704R00023